VARANASI GUIDE

Varanasi for the First-Time Traveler: Awakening the Soul in India's Sacred City

Dr. DONALD A. JOHNSON

Copyright ©

Copyright © 2026 by Dr. Donald A. Johnson

All rights reserved. No part of this publication may be reproduced, distributed, or transmitted in any form or by any means, including photocopying, recording, or other electronic or mechanical methods, without the prior written permission of the publisher, except in the case of brief quotations embodied in critical reviews and certain other noncommercial uses permitted by copyright law.

This book is a work of creative nonfiction. While every effort has been made to ensure accuracy at the time of writing, travel details such as schedules, prices, and regulations are subject to change. The author and publisher assume no responsibility for the accuracy, timeliness, or completeness of the information contained herein and shall not be held liable for any loss or damages arising from its use. Travelers are encouraged to verify details independently before making plans.

Disclaimer

This book is intended as a general travel guide and cultural resource. While every effort has been made to provide accurate and up-to-date information at the time of publication, details such as transportation schedules, prices, accommodations, and local regulations are subject to change without notice.

The author and publisher make no representations or warranties with respect to the accuracy, completeness, or suitability of the contents of this guide and shall not be held liable for any damages, losses, or inconveniences that may arise in connection with the use of this book.

Travel, cultural experiences, and participation in local traditions are undertaken at the reader's own discretion and risk. Readers are encouraged to verify critical details directly with service providers and official sources prior to making travel arrangements.

This guide is for informational purposes only and does not replace professional advice in matters of health, safety, or legal requirements.

Acknowledgments

Writing Varanasi Travel Guide 2026 has been a journey of both research and heart, and it would not have been possible without the support and inspiration of many.

I would like to express my deepest gratitude to the people of Varanasi, whose warmth, spirituality, and timeless traditions opened the doors of this sacred city to me. Their generosity and stories are the soul of this book.

To fellow travelers, photographers, and cultural guides who shared their insights and experiences—thank you for reminding me that every journey is richer when voices are shared.

Special thanks to my family and loved ones for their patience, encouragement, and unwavering belief in my work. Your support fuels my writing.

Finally, to you, dear reader: thank you for choosing this guide as your companion. May your time in

Varanasi be filled with discovery, peace, and inspiration.

— Dr. Donald A. Johnson

Table of contents

Chapter 1: Welcome to Varanasi – City of Eternal Light
    The Spirit of Kashi: Why Varanasi Endures Through Time
    Varanasi in 2026: Tradition Meets the Modern Traveler

Chapter 2: Preparing for Your Journey
    Best Time to Visit: Seasons, Festivals, and Weather
    Travel Essentials: Documents, Currency, and Connectivity

Chapter 3: Arriving in the Holy City
    Getting There: Flights, Trains, and Road Routes
    Navigating the City: Rickshaws, Boats, and Walking the Alleys

Chapter 4: Where to Stay – From Hostels to Haveli Hotels
    Budget-Friendly Accommodations: Guesthouses & Backpacker Hostels
    Luxury by the Ganges: Heritage Hotels and Boutique Retreats

Chapter 5: The Ghats of Varanasi – Steps into Eternity
    The Iconic Ghats: Dasashwamedh, Manikarnika, and Assi
    Hidden Ghats: Quiet Corners Along the River

Chapter 6: Sacred Rituals and Spiritual Awakening
    Witnessing the Ganga Aarti: An Evening of Light and Devotion
    Life and Death on the Ghats: Cremation Rituals and Eternal Flame

Chapter 7: Temples, Shrines, and Sacred Spaces

- Kashi Vishwanath Temple: Heartbeat of Hindu Faith
- Beyond the Famous: Lesser-Known Temples and Shrines

Chapter 8: Cultural Treasures of Banaras
- Music, Dance, and the Banaras Gharana
- Handwoven Magic: Banarasi Silk and Craft Traditions

Chapter 9: A Culinary Pilgrimage
- Street Food Delights: Chaat, Lassi, and Kachori
- Dining with a View: Riverside Cafés and Rooftop Restaurants

Chapter 10: Festivals of Fire and Color
- Dev Deepawali: The Festival of a Thousand Lamps
- Holi in Banaras: Colors of Joy and Spiritual Play

Chapter 11: Day Trips and Excursions Beyond Varanasi
- Sarnath: In the Footsteps of the Buddha
- Rural Escapes: Villages, Weaving Centers, and Countryside Life

Chapter 12: Modern Varanasi – 2026 and Beyond
- Smart City Developments: Infrastructure and Traveler Experience
- Balancing Tourism with Tradition: Sustainable and Responsible Travel

Chapter 13: Reflections – Leaving with the Spirit of Varanasi
- Lessons from the Ghats: What Varanasi Teaches Travelers
- Taking the Light Home: Carrying Varanasi Into Everyday Life

Introduction

Varanasi is not just a place you visit — it's a place that visits you.
Here, dawn breaks over the Ganges like a hymn, the ghats echo with chants and bells, and the air carries centuries of devotion, mystery, and resilience. For millennia, seekers, poets, pilgrims, and wanderers have come to this ancient city searching for meaning, and in 2026, it remains as timeless and transformative as ever.

This guide has been created to help you step into Varanasi with both eyes open and heart ready. Whether you are drawn by the sacred rituals along the riverbanks, the labyrinth of narrow alleys filled with vibrant life, or the deep silence of an early morning boat ride, Varanasi offers more than sights — it offers experiences that stay with you long after you've left.

Inside these pages, you will find everything you need to navigate this sacred city with confidence:

Practical guidance on when to go, where to stay, how to get around, and what to expect.

Insider insights into the city's temples, rituals, festivals, cuisine, and hidden gems.

Cultural wisdom and reflections that help you connect with Varanasi not only as a traveler but as a participant in its living story.

Travel in 2026 is about more than ticking destinations off a list. It's about traveling with intention, respect, and curiosity. Varanasi rewards such travelers richly, with moments that surprise, challenge, and transform.

This is more than a guidebook. It's an invitation — to walk the ghats, listen to the rhythms of sitars and temple bells, savor street food under the stars, and allow yourself to be changed by the city that has been called the heart of India's soul.

Welcome to Varanasi Travel Guide 2026.
May this book be your trusted companion as you discover one of the world's oldest and most extraordinary cities.

This introduction balances practical promise with emotional pull, so readers know they're holding something more than a checklist — they're about to embark on a soul-journey.

Chapter 1: Welcome to Varanasi – City of Eternal Light

The Spirit of Kashi: Why Varanasi Endures Through Time

To step into Varanasi is to step into eternity. Known also as Kashi — "the City of Light" — it is believed to be one of the oldest continuously inhabited cities in the world. For over 3,000 years, life here has revolved around the sacred river Ganges, where dawn rituals, funerary fires, chanting priests, and everyday human stories unfold in an unbroken rhythm. Unlike other cities that measure themselves by progress and modernity, Varanasi measures itself by continuity.

What makes Varanasi unique among the world's cities is not just its age, but its unwavering devotion to the sacred. Empires have risen and fallen, yet the city has remained the spiritual heart of India. It is said that Lord Shiva himself founded Kashi, and to die here is to achieve liberation from the cycle of rebirth. This belief has drawn millions of pilgrims who come to bathe in the Ganges, perform ancestral rites, or simply feel the divine pulse of the city.

Through the centuries, Varanasi has shaped the world's religion, culture, and philosophy. It was here that the Upanishads were composed, shaping Hindu thought for millennia. It was here that the Buddha preached his first sermon in nearby Sarnath, planting the seeds of a new religion. Saints, poets, and mystics — from Kabir to Tulsidas — sang of truth and devotion in its lanes, giving India some of its most enduring spiritual literature. Even today, the Banaras Gharana of music carries forward centuries of melody, while silk weavers continue ancient crafts that once clothed royalty.

For the traveler arriving for the first time, Varanasi is often overwhelming — a collision of chaos and divinity. Narrow alleys swirl with incense, temple bells, and the cries of vendors. The ghats reveal life in its rawest form: children playing by the river, sadhus in meditation, families releasing flower offerings, and funeral pyres blazing as a reminder of mortality. Some travelers describe awe, others confusion, but most feel an undeniable sense of being drawn into something far greater than themselves.

Varanasi endures because it is more than a city — it is a living prayer. It holds up a mirror to humanity's eternal search for meaning, reminding each visitor that life is both fleeting and sacred. To walk its ghats is to touch the heartbeat of India, and perhaps, the timeless rhythm of the universe itself.

This version blends history, culture, spirituality, and emotion — giving your readers both knowledge and atmosphere.

Varanasi in 2026: Tradition Meets the Modern Traveler

Varanasi has long been a city where the past and present coexist in a delicate, mesmerizing balance. By 2026, this timeless city has embraced several modern developments designed to make travel smoother while preserving its spiritual soul.

Traveler-Friendly Upgrades

Connectivity: High-speed Wi-Fi zones now cover major ghats, popular markets, and key temples, allowing travelers to share experiences instantly without disconnecting from the sacred atmosphere.

Transportation: App-based e-rickshaws, taxis, and ride-sharing services have become widely available, offering safe and convenient ways to navigate the narrow, winding streets of the old city.

Digital Guides & Apps: Smartphone apps like Kashi Connect provide live temple schedules, guided tours, cultural insights, and even digital maps to avoid getting lost in the labyrinthine alleys.

Eco-Initiatives: Solar-powered streetlights along the ghats, river-cleaning campaigns, and sustainable waste management are making Varanasi a more environmentally conscious destination.

Living Traditions Amid Modernity

Despite these advances, Varanasi's spiritual heart remains untouched. Ancient rituals continue uninterrupted, and pilgrims still gather for Ganga Aarti, morning prayers, and centuries-old ceremonies. Modern conveniences exist not to replace tradition but to support it—making it accessible to travelers without diminishing its authenticity.

Example Contrasts in 2026:

At Dasashwamedh Ghat, priests perform the evening Ganga Aarti under the soft glow of flames, while tourists nearby quietly capture the ceremony on smartphones and drones.

A modern café with rooftop seating and Wi-Fi sits just a few alleys away from a centuries-old temple, where saffron-robed monks chant and devotees offer flowers. Patrons sip artisanal chai, absorbing the aroma of incense drifting in from the sacred space next door.

Digital kiosks at major ghats provide historical context and safety tips, guiding travelers through rituals they might otherwise misunderstand.

Traveler Takeaway:
By 2026, Varanasi is not a city frozen in time, nor a modern metropolis stripped of its soul—it is a living dialogue between past and present. First-time visitors will find that technology, comfort, and modern conveniences enhance their experience without overshadowing the eternal spirit that has drawn pilgrims for millennia.

Chapter 2: Preparing for Your Journey

Best Time to Visit: Seasons, Festivals, and Weather

Varanasi is a city that never sleeps and never pauses — each season dresses the ghats, the alleys, and the river in a new mood. To know when to visit is not just about comfort, but also about what kind of experience you wish to carry home.

Winter (October – March): Cool, Crisp, and Festive

Winter is the most popular time to visit Varanasi. Days are mild and pleasant, with temperatures ranging from 12°C to 25°C (54°F to 77°F). Mornings on the river feel mystical, with a soft mist hanging over the water as boats glide silently through the fog. Evenings are cool, perfect for wandering the ghats or sitting by a rooftop café with chai in hand.

Festivals in Winter 2026:

Dev Deepawali (November): The ghats glow with millions of diyas, a once-in-a-lifetime sight.

Ganga Mahotsav (usually in November): A cultural festival celebrating music, dance, and river traditions.

Makar Sankranti (January): Celebrated with kite flying and ritual bathing in the Ganges.

Packing tips: Bring light layers for the day and warm sweaters or shawls for evenings by the river. Comfortable walking shoes are essential, as you'll spend much of your time on foot. A scarf or pashmina is useful both for warmth and temple etiquette.

Summer (April – June): Intense Heat, Slower Rhythms

Summer in Varanasi is not for the faint-hearted. Temperatures soar up to 40°C (104°F), with dry, blazing afternoons that seem to pause even the bustling city. Life slows down, and locals retreat indoors during midday, leaving the ghats quieter than usual. Early mornings and evenings become the best times to explore, when the golden light softens the heat.

Festivals in Summer 2026:

Ramnagar Ramlila (depending on the lunar calendar, sometimes extends into April): A dramatic, month-long staging of the Ramayana across the river in Ramnagar.

Religious fairs and smaller rituals continue, but summer is less festival-heavy.

Packing tips: Light, breathable cotton clothing is a must. Carry sunscreen, sunglasses, and a wide-brimmed hat for protection. A reusable water bottle with a filtration system is invaluable. Sandals or airy shoes will keep you comfortable, but avoid open footwear when walking in crowded or muddy lanes.

Monsoon (July – September): Lush, Wet, and Dramatic

The monsoon transforms Varanasi into a city of contrasts. Heavy rains swell the Ganges, covering many of the lower ghats. Thunderstorms roll in suddenly, then pass, leaving behind shimmering streets and vibrant skies. While the rain can disrupt boat rides and make travel less predictable, it also brings a sense of drama and renewal to the city. Crowds are thinner, and for the adventurous, monsoon offers an unusually intimate glimpse of life by the river.

Festivals in Monsoon 2026:

Nag Panchami (July/August): A festival honoring the serpent gods, with rituals performed in temples.

Shravan Month (July/August): A holy period dedicated to Lord Shiva, attracting waves of pilgrims.

Packing tips: Pack a lightweight rain jacket, umbrella, and quick-dry clothing. Waterproof sandals or shoes with good grip are useful for navigating slippery ghats. Keep electronics and valuables in waterproof pouches. Patience is key, as rain may delay plans.

Choosing the Right Season for You

If you seek festivals, energy, and ideal weather, winter is your season.

If you prefer quiet ghats and fewer crowds, brave the heat of summer.

If you love atmospheric drama and don't mind getting wet, monsoon will show you Varanasi at its most raw and soulful.

No matter when you come, Varanasi will meet you with both challenges and wonders. Pack wisely, come prepared, and let the city reveal its different faces through the turning of the seasons.

This gives readers:

A sensory journey of each season.

Festival highlights for 2026 to help them plan.

Packing checklists they'll find practical and reassuring.

Travel Essentials: Documents, Currency, and Connectivity

Before setting out for Varanasi, having your paperwork, money management, and digital access sorted will ensure a smooth experience. In 2026, India has streamlined many of its travel processes, making it easier than ever for international visitors to arrive prepared.

Travel Documents, Visas, and Permits

Passport: Your passport must be valid for at least six months beyond your intended stay, with at least two blank pages.

Visa Requirements:

Most travelers will need an Indian tourist visa. The widely used e-Visa system remains in place in 2026, available for 30-day, 90-day, or 1-year multiple-entry stays. Applications are done online and processed quickly.

Nationals of certain countries enjoy visa-on-arrival privileges (check the updated list on the Government of India's official portal).

Special Permits: Varanasi itself requires no extra permits, but if you plan excursions to border regions or sensitive areas, additional permissions may be necessary.

Travel Insurance: Strongly recommended. Policies covering health, theft, and trip disruptions are invaluable, especially in a city where the unexpected often becomes part of the journey.

Currency and Money Matters

Currency: The local currency is the Indian Rupee (INR). ATMs are widely available across Varanasi, especially in tourist and commercial areas.

Cash vs Digital Payments:

Cash remains king in smaller shops, temples, and street food stalls. Carry small denominations (₹10, ₹20, ₹50, ₹100) for easy transactions.

Digital payments have become mainstream in 2026, even in local tea stalls, through apps like UPI, Google Pay, Paytm, and PhonePe. International travelers can link their credit/debit cards to UPI wallets for seamless transactions.

Exchanging Money:

Currency exchange counters are available at the airport and major banks, though ATMs typically provide better rates.

Stick to authorized exchange services to avoid counterfeit notes.

Credit/Debit Cards: Widely accepted at hotels, restaurants, and larger stores. Visa and Mastercard are most reliable.

Tip: Keep a mix of digital payment options, cards, and cash. While India is rapidly becoming cashless, the spiritual heart of Varanasi still thrives in rupee notes passed from palm to palm.

Connectivity: Staying Connected in 2026

Mobile & Data:

Varanasi now enjoys strong 5G coverage in most areas, making video calls and streaming easy.

International visitors can choose between a local SIM card (available at the airport or city shops with passport verification) or an eSIM, which can be purchased online before arrival and activated instantly.

Top providers include Jio, Airtel, and Vi (Vodafone Idea), all offering affordable prepaid data packs.

Wi-Fi:

Free Wi-Fi hotspots are available at major ghats, tourist areas, cafés, and hotels.

Speeds are generally good, but may slow during peak hours.

Practical Tip: While connectivity is reliable, remember that Varanasi's power cuts and overloaded networks can occasionally disrupt service. Carry a portable power bank and download offline maps of the city as a backup.

Final Word for the Traveler

With the right documents in hand, a smart mix of cash and digital payments, and a reliable mobile connection, you'll find navigating Varanasi far smoother than travelers did even a decade ago. Yet, don't forget to occasionally disconnect: put away the phone, step off the digital map, and let the city guide you the old way — by sound, sight, and intuition.

This section blends practical checklists with a touch of atmosphere, making it both useful and inspiring.

Chapter 3: Arriving in the Holy City

Getting There: Flights, Trains, and Road Routes

Varanasi, often described as the beating spiritual heart of India, is surprisingly well-connected to the rest of the country—and increasingly to the world. By 2026, improved air routes, upgraded rail corridors, and expanded highways have made reaching the city easier, faster, and more comfortable than ever.

By Air: Flying into Varanasi

Lal Bahadur Shastri International Airport (VNS):

Located about 22 km from the city center, Varanasi's airport is the most convenient gateway for international and domestic travelers.

By 2026, the airport has undergone a terminal expansion, increasing international connectivity. Direct flights now link Varanasi with hubs such as Dubai, Bangkok, Singapore, Kathmandu, and London (seasonal charter routes).

Domestically, frequent flights connect Varanasi with Delhi, Mumbai, Kolkata, Hyderabad, Bengaluru, and Jaipur.

Travel Tips:

Book flights well in advance during festival periods like Dev Deepawali and Holi, when demand spikes.

Prepaid taxis, app-based rides (Ola, Uber), and shuttle buses connect the airport to the city, though traffic can stretch a 45-minute ride into 90 minutes at peak hours.

By Train: Riding India's Lifeline

Varanasi Junction (Varanasi Cantt Station): The city's main station, buzzing with life day and night, serves as a hub for trains from every corner of India.

Manduadih (Banaras Station): A modernized alternative to the main junction, now streamlined for premium services.

Mughal Sarai (Pt. Deen Dayal Upadhyaya Junction): A major rail junction 18 km away, connecting long-distance trains.

Upgrades by 2026:

High-speed rail corridors now shorten travel times between Delhi and Varanasi to under 4 hours, making train travel not just economical but competitive with flying.

Enhanced onboard Wi-Fi, cleaner coaches, and app-based seat bookings make rail journeys more comfortable.

Travel Tips:

Use the official IRCTC app or trusted platforms for bookings—avoid touts at the station.

Book AC-class tickets for overnight journeys, which offer better comfort and security.

Trains are ideal for those wanting to soak up India's landscapes at a slower pace.

By Road: Highways and Scenic Routes

National Highways:

The Varanasi–Lucknow Expressway (newly operational in 2025) has cut travel time to just over 3 hours.

Highways now link Varanasi more efficiently with Allahabad (Prayagraj), Patna, Bodh Gaya, and Gorakhpur.

Buses & Coaches: State-run and private luxury buses connect Varanasi with neighboring cities. Online booking portals ensure safe, reliable services.

Car Rentals & Taxis: Popular for those wishing to combine Varanasi with nearby spiritual hubs like Sarnath (10 km) or Ayodhya (200 km).

Travel Tips:

Road trips offer flexibility, but expect chaotic traffic inside Varanasi itself. Park outside the old city and walk or take cycle rickshaws.

Night driving is not advised due to unpredictable road conditions.

Budget & Booking Tips

Flights: Book at least 2–3 months in advance for festival season; midweek flights are generally cheaper.

Trains: Secure your ticket early; India's railways sell out fast, especially sleeper berths.

Buses: Apps like RedBus, AbhiBus, or state-run portals are reliable for online reservations.

General Tip: Always cross-check routes and reviews online before booking—this small step ensures safety and avoids scams.

Final Thought

No matter how you arrive—gliding down from the clouds, rattling in on a train, or navigating highways—the approach to Varanasi feels like a passage into another dimension. The hum of modern travel fades as the city's ancient chants and temple bells greet you, reminding every traveler that they've entered not just a destination, but a living legend.

This gives a well-rounded mix of practical logistics and emotional pull.

Navigating the City: Rickshaws, Boats, and Walking the Alleys

Moving around Varanasi is as much a part of the experience as visiting its temples and ghats. The city's rhythm is slow yet chaotic, sacred yet noisy, timeless yet very real. By 2026, modern apps and improved infrastructure have made getting around easier, but the true magic of Varanasi still lies in its rickshaws, boats, and labyrinthine alleys.

Walking the Alleys: Into the Living Soul of Kashi

The Experience:

The old city of Varanasi is a maze of winding alleys barely wide enough for two people to pass. Cows, scooters, pilgrims, and vendors all compete for space, creating a sensory overload of incense, bells, laughter, and holy chants.

Each turn reveals something new—a hidden shrine, a local sweet shop, or a sudden opening to the vast sweep of the Ganges.

Traveler Tips:

Wear comfortable shoes; the uneven cobblestones and occasional muddy patches can be challenging.

Google Maps often struggles in these tiny lanes; follow landmarks or ask locals with a smile.

Early mornings are quieter and more peaceful; afternoons are bustling with activity.

Rickshaws: The Pulse of Everyday Life

Cycle Rickshaws: Still the most traditional and eco-friendly way to get around short distances. They move slowly, allowing you to soak up the sights.

Auto Rickshaws (Tuk-Tuks): Ideal for slightly longer journeys within the city. They're faster and easier to hail via apps like Ola or Uber in 2026, though bargaining remains common.

Traveler Tips:

Always agree on a fare before starting, unless using an app.

Expect short trips within the city to cost ₹50–₹200 depending on distance and time.

For fairness, avoid aggressive bargaining—rounding up a little is appreciated by drivers.

Rickshaws are not just transport; they're storytellers. Many drivers share tales of festivals, family, or city legends if you ask politely.

Boats on the Ganges: The Heartbeat of Varanasi

Sunrise Ride:

The Ganges at dawn is pure magic. The first light touches the temples, priests chant mantras, and pilgrims dip in the sacred waters. Birds swoop overhead, and the city awakens in golden silence broken only by the oar's rhythm.

Sunset Ride:

Equally mesmerizing, sunset rides give front-row seats to the Ganga Aarti ceremony at Dashashwamedh Ghat, when hundreds of lamps are offered to the river. The air glows with fire, chanting, and the fragrance of sandalwood.

Practical Tips:

Boat rides can be rowboats, motorboats, or group cruises. Rowboats are quieter and more atmospheric; motorboats are faster but noisier.

Expect to pay ₹300–₹600 per person for a 60-minute ride; prices rise during festivals.

Always confirm the duration of the ride in advance.

Life jackets are increasingly available (required for licensed operators by 2026). Choose operators who comply with safety measures.

Cultural Etiquette for Travelers

Be patient: Crowds and delays are part of the Varanasi experience.

Dress modestly, especially near temples and ghats. Shoulders and knees covered show respect.

Avoid photographing people bathing in the Ganges without permission—it's a deeply personal ritual.

Offer small tips to boatmen or rickshaw drivers if service is good; it goes a long way in supporting local livelihoods.

Final Thought

Navigating Varanasi isn't just about moving from place to place—it's about moving through layers of history, spirituality, and humanity. Whether you're gliding on the sacred river, jolting along in a rickshaw, or getting blissfully lost in the alleys, every journey is a reminder that in this city, the path itself is as meaningful as the destination.

Chapter 4: Where to Stay – From Hostels to Haveli Hotels

Budget-Friendly Accommodations: Guesthouses & Backpacker Hostels

For travelers arriving in Varanasi with a backpack, a journal, and a thirst for authentic connection, budget accommodations are more than just a place to rest—they're a gateway to community and culture. By 2026, the city's budget-friendly stays have become a vibrant ecosystem that blends traditional Indian hospitality with the laid-back global backpacker spirit.

The Vibe of a Backpacker Hostel in Varanasi

Hostels in Varanasi are not just about cheap beds—they're about stories exchanged over chai, rooftop jam sessions with the Ganges as a backdrop, and friendships that form over sunrise boat rides.

Expect dorm-style bunks, shared bathrooms, and common lounges with colorful murals, yoga mats, and shelves stacked with travel-worn books.

Many hostels adopt an eco-conscious ethos in 2026—think solar-powered heating, filtered water stations to reduce plastic waste, and vegetarian communal kitchens.

The rhythm of life is easy: travelers swap tips about the best street food, debate spirituality after attending an Aarti, or gather to watch the evening lamps flicker across the river.

Best Areas for Budget Travelers

1. Assi Ghat – A backpacker favorite.

Known for its lively cafés, yoga centers, and music nights.

Many guesthouses and hostels here are just steps from the river, making it easy to start your day with a sunrise walk.

2. Dashashwamedh Ghat Area – Right at the cultural heart.

Bustling, busy, and a little overwhelming—but perfect if you want to be close to the Ganga Aarti and old city action.

Guesthouses here offer unbeatable access to temples and street food.

3. Godowlia & Chowk – For those who love chaos.

Narrow lanes filled with spice markets and sari shops.

Guesthouses here are smaller, family-run, and deeply traditional—ideal if you want immersion over comfort.

Social Experiences Offered by Hostels & Guesthouses

Cooking Classes: Learn to prepare classics like banarasi kachori, lassi, or a simple dal-tadka from a local cook. These classes often end in shared meals on the rooftop.

Walking Tours: Many hostels organize guided tours through the old city lanes, highlighting hidden temples, silk weavers' workshops, and local sweet shops.

Boat Ride Packages: Coordinated sunrise and sunset rides with other hostel guests—cheaper, safer, and more fun as a group.

Yoga & Meditation Sessions: Morning yoga on the rooftop, sometimes led by local teachers, provides a serene start before diving into the city's chaos.

Cultural Nights: From sitar recitals to storytelling circles where travelers share personal journeys, these nights foster an atmosphere of camaraderie.

Practical Tips for Budget Travelers

Dorm beds typically range from ₹500–₹1,000 per night ($6–$12) in 2026, while private budget rooms are around ₹1,500–₹2,500 ($18–$30).

Book in advance during major festivals like Dev Deepawali or Holi, as hostels fill quickly.

Always check if the price includes essentials like Wi-Fi, breakfast, and hot showers.

Look for hostels with strong community reviews—"clean bathrooms" and "helpful staff" are worth more than fancy décor.

Final Thought

Budget accommodations in Varanasi offer something beyond affordability—they provide belonging. In these lively hostels and family-run guesthouses, the city comes alive not just through sights and sounds but through the connections you make. For many travelers, the friendships formed here last far longer than their stay.

Luxury by the Ganges: Heritage Hotels and Boutique Retreats

For travelers seeking more than comfort—those who want immersion wrapped in elegance—Varanasi's luxury stays are unlike anywhere else. In 2026, the city's historic riverside havelis (traditional mansions) and boutique retreats have become sanctuaries where old-world charm meets modern sophistication, offering an unforgettable lens into the soul of the Ganges.

The Charm of Riverside Havelis

Imagine stepping through carved wooden doors into a courtyard filled with mango trees, listening to the faint echo of temple bells across the river. These restored heritage havelis, once homes of nobles and merchants, now serve as boutique hotels that honor Varanasi's architectural legacy.

Interiors are a blend of antique furniture, silk drapes woven by local artisans, and marble courtyards softened by candlelight. Every detail—from brass oil lamps to intricately painted ceilings—whispers stories of centuries past.

Staying in a riverside haveli isn't just about luxury; it's about living in history, with the Ganges flowing silently at your doorstep.

Luxury with Sustainability in 2026

By 2026, many high-end hotels in Varanasi will embrace eco-luxury—a philosophy that ensures indulgence without guilt.

Solar panels and rainwater harvesting systems are standard features, while natural cooling techniques inspired by traditional design reduce reliance on air-conditioning.

Gourmet restaurants inside these hotels increasingly focus on farm-to-table menus, featuring organic produce sourced from nearby villages.

Some boutique retreats even sponsor Ganga clean-up initiatives, inviting guests to participate in eco-conscious cultural activities. Luxury here is no longer about excess—it's about responsibility with refinement.

The Best Views in Town

Few experiences rival the privilege of waking up to the first light shimmering across the Ganges or watching the famed Ganga Aarti from your private balcony. In 2026, these are among the most coveted vantage points:

BrijRama Palace – Perhaps Varanasi's most iconic heritage hotel, this 18th-century palace offers unmatched views of Dashashwamedh Ghat, where the evening Aarti unfolds in its full grandeur. Guests can sip masala chai while watching the city's spiritual heartbeat come alive.

Taj Ganges, Varanasi – Set within lush gardens, this property blends global standards of luxury with quiet Indian elegance. Its curated sunrise experiences include boat rides arranged directly by the hotel.

Amritara Suryauday Haveli – Known for intimate charm, this boutique retreat at Shivala Ghat provides front-row seats to both sunrise and evening boat processions, with fewer crowds than the central ghats.

Independent Boutique Retreats – In 2026, newer boutique hotels—often run by designers or heritage enthusiasts—are rising along quieter stretches of the river, offering luxury without the bustle of the main ghats.

Practical Luxury Tips for Travelers

Book early for festival season: Dev Deepawali and Holi reservations at riverside luxury hotels often fill up months in advance.

Expect nightly rates from ₹12,000–₹40,000 ($150–$500), depending on exclusivity and river views.

Many properties now include personalized spiritual experiences—private puja arrangements, guided meditation, or even silk-weaving workshops.

Dress modestly when stepping outside the hotel, even if you're enjoying five-star comfort—remember, you're in India's holiest city.

Final Thought

To stay in a heritage haveli or boutique retreat by the Ganges is to experience Varanasi at its most sublime intersection of the past and present. Here, the luxury lies not only in soft linens and curated menus, but in the privilege of witnessing the eternal flow of the river—where spirituality and serenity meet.

Chapter 5: The Ghats of Varanasi – Steps into Eternity

The Iconic Ghats: Dasashwamedh, Manikarnika, and Assi

To walk along the ghats of Varanasi is to enter a living tapestry where life, death, and devotion coexist seamlessly. Each ghat has its own personality, rhythm, and story, yet together they form the sacred spine of the city. Among the nearly

90 ghats, three stand out as the most iconic: Dasashwamedh, Manikarnika, and Assi.

Dasashwamedh Ghat – The Spiritual Theater of Varanasi

The Experience: Arriving here feels like stepping into the city's central stage. At sunrise, pilgrims bathe in the river, offering prayers with folded hands, while priests chant mantras over brass lamps. By evening, the ghat transforms into a grand spiritual spectacle—the world-famous Ganga Aarti.

Rituals & Sights: Priests in saffron robes raise blazing oil lamps in choreographed movements, bells ring, conch shells echo, and thousands of devotees join in chants. This devotion turned into performance, where the Ganga herself is worshiped as a goddess.

Traveler's Role:

The respectful way to experience the Aarti is to arrive early, sit quietly among the crowd, and absorb the energy without pushing for the "best seat."

Photographs are allowed, but avoid blocking rituals or using flash.

Many travelers hire a boat to watch the ceremony from the river, gaining a unique, floating perspective.

Manikarnika Ghat – Where Life Meets Death

The Experience: Perhaps the most powerful and unsettling of all ghats, Manikarnika is the city's principal cremation ground. Fires here burn 24 hours a day, believed to grant moksha—freedom from the cycle of rebirth—to those cremated on its banks.

Rituals & Sights:

Families gather to perform final rites, the sacred fire is lit, and bodies wrapped in vibrant silks are carried down to the steps. The smell of sandalwood mingles with the smoke of pyres, creating an atmosphere that is both solemn and eternal.

Above the ghat, stacks of firewood tower high, ready to fuel the endless cycle of life's ending.

Traveler's Role:

Witness with deep respect and silence—this is no place for casual chatter or intrusive photography.

Guides may offer insights into Hindu beliefs about death and liberation, helping travelers understand the profound spiritual weight of the site.

If uncomfortable, travelers can also observe from a boat, which provides distance while still offering a glimpse into this sacred passage.

Assi Ghat – The Soul of Varanasi's Morning

The Experience: Assi Ghat, where the Ganga meets the Assi River, is where locals and travelers alike greet the day. It is the city's most welcoming and lively ghat, especially at dawn.

Rituals & Sights:

The daily Subah-e-Banaras (Morning of Varanasi) program fills the ghat with classical music, yoga sessions, and devotional chants. Watching the sunrise here while hundreds of people practice yoga by the river is a transformative experience.

Later in the day, Assi becomes a hub for students, artists, and curious travelers—a place to sip chai, listen to folk musicians, and exchange stories.

Traveler's Role:

Join a morning yoga class or simply sit on the steps with a cup of steaming tea and watch the world awaken.

Travelers are welcome to participate in rituals here—lighting a small diya (lamp) and setting it afloat on the water is a simple yet powerful gesture.

Evenings bring a smaller, more intimate version of the Ganga Aarti, perfect for those seeking a less crowded experience than Dasashwamedh.

Final Thought

Standing on these three ghats—Dasashwamedh's grandeur, Manikarnika's intensity, and Assi's serenity—a traveler witnesses the full spectrum of Varanasi. Together, they reveal the city's eternal rhythm: celebration, departure, and renewal.

Hidden Ghats: Quiet Corners Along the River

While the major ghats hum with rituals, festivals, and endless crowds, Varanasi also shelters quieter steps leading into the Ganga—hidden that's where time slows down, silence deepens, and the city reveals its private face. For travelers willing to wander away from the main thoroughfare, these corners provide rare moments of reflection and connection.

Raja Ghat – Serenity in Stone

Atmosphere: Once part of an old palace complex, Raja Ghat is more contemplative than ceremonial. Its weathered stone steps lead to tranquil waters where only a few locals come to bathe or wash clothes.

Unique Story: Built by a royal family centuries ago, it carries whispers of regal patronage yet feels abandoned to time.

Traveler's Tip: Visit just after sunrise—the soft light makes the stone glow, and reflections on the water create stunning photography opportunities without interruption.

Kedar Ghat – The South's Sacred Touch

Atmosphere: Often overlooked by foreign tourists, Kedar Ghat is a favorite among South Indian pilgrims. Painted in vivid blues and reds, it carries the distinct flavor of Tamil rituals and prayers.

Unique Story: The ghat is home to the Kedareswara Shiva temple, considered one of the holiest shrines for devotees from southern India.

The chants here sound different—adding to the layered music of Varanasi.

Traveler's Tip: Photograph the temple's painted backdrop against the morning rituals—it creates a frame filled with culture, devotion, and color.

Harishchandra Ghat – Fire Without Fame

Atmosphere: Like Manikarnika, this is a cremation ghat, but smaller, quieter, and often overlooked. Its fires burn steadily, less crowded, more intimate.

Unique Story: Named after the legendary king Harishchandra, who symbolized truth and sacrifice, this ghat carries a deep moral resonance. Local lore says those cremated here also attain moksha.

Traveler's Tip: Best observed respectfully from a boat at dusk. The faint glow of fire against the darkening sky creates one of the most hauntingly beautiful scenes on the river.

Tulsi Ghat – Where Poetry Breathes

Atmosphere: A calm, scholarly ghat with fewer rituals and more quiet contemplation.

Unique Story: It is named after the poet-saint Tulsidas, who composed parts of the Ramcharitmanas here. Literary pilgrims still come to sit on its steps, reading verses in silence.

Traveler's Tip: Carry a notebook. This is a place for journaling, sketching, or quiet reflection. In the golden hour, the play of shadows on the steps makes it a dreamy spot for intimate photography.

Chousatti Ghat – The Hidden Goddess

Atmosphere: Nestled between busier ghats, this quiet corner is home to shrines of 64 Yoginis, making it a spot infused with mysticism.

Unique Story: It's said that visiting this ghat pleases the divine feminine energy, and pilgrims often stop here quietly for blessings before moving on.

Traveler's Tip: Look for early morning incense smoke rising against the ghat's shrines—it's a photographer's dream.

Moments of Reflection

The hidden ghats invite you to:

Pause with a cup of chai, away from the crowd's roar.

Sketch or photograph locals as they go about daily life.

Meditate by the water, feeling the subtle rhythm of the city rather than its booming heartbeat.

Final Thought

The hidden ghats of Varanasi remind travelers that the city is not only about grand rituals and fiery symbolism, but also about whispers, quiet devotion, and unnoticed beauty. To find them is to discover Varanasi's soul in solitude.

Chapter 6: Sacred Rituals and Spiritual Awakening

Witnessing the Ganga Aarti: An Evening of Light and Devotion

As the sun sets and the first shadows stretch across the sacred river, Varanasi transforms into a theater of devotion. The Ganga Aarti—performed every evening at Dasashwamedh Ghat and Assi Ghat—is not just a ritual, but a breathtaking choreography of fire, sound, and reverence that binds locals and travelers in collective awe.

The Sensory Tapestry

Sound: The air vibrates with the rhythmic chanting of Sanskrit mantras, accompanied by the deep clang of temple bells and the low hum of conch shells. Each note seems to ripple across the river, carried by the night breeze.

Sight: Priests dressed in saffron and cream robes move in unison, lifting large brass lamps that sway in sweeping arcs. Flames spiral into the night sky, illuminating the faces of thousands gathered along the ghats.

Smell: The aroma of burning incense mingles with marigold garlands and the earthy scent of the river. Together, they create a heady perfume that feels ancient and timeless.

Feeling: For many, it is a moment of stillness within chaos—a sense that something greater is unfolding, both around them and within them.

How to Experience the Aarti

From the Ghat (Ground Level): Standing among the crowds gives you a raw, immersive feel—the chants echo in your bones, and the energy is palpable. Be prepared for tight spaces, but also for the intimacy of being shoulder-to-shoulder with devotees.

By Boat on the Ganges: Watching from the water offers serenity and perspective. The reflection of the flames dances on the river, and the sound seems to float across the current. It's less crowded and deeply meditative.

From a Rooftop Café or Terrace: Perfect for travelers who want to avoid the crush of the crowd. You gain a panoramic view, with the ghats, priests, and river spread before you like a grand stage.

Etiquette for Respectful Observation

Dress Modestly: Out of respect for the sacred setting, wear clothing that covers shoulders and knees.

Photography: Discreet photography is allowed, but avoid using flash or stepping in front of worshippers. The Aarti is not a show—it is prayer.

Participate Mindfully: You don't have to be Hindu to join in the devotion. Place your hands together in namaste or simply observe quietly with reverence.

Offering Rituals: Locals often float small lamps (diyas) with marigold flowers on the river as a prayer for blessings. Travelers are welcome to do the same, but always with mindfulness to avoid littering.

A Lasting Impression

To witness the Ganga Aarti is to watch light triumph over darkness—a ritual that has been performed for generations and will continue for centuries more. Many travelers leave with tears in their eyes, carrying the glow of this moment long after they have departed Varanasi.

It is not merely something you see—it is something you feel, etched into memory as one of the city's most profound gifts.

Life and Death on the Ghats: Cremation Rituals and Eternal Flame

Varanasi is not only a city of light—it is a city of endings and beginnings. On the sacred banks of the Ganges, life and death meet without fear or shame. Here, the rituals of cremation are not hidden away but performed in the open, reminding every traveler that mortality is not an end, but a passage.

The Significance of Cremation in Varanasi

At Manikarnika Ghat and Harishchandra Ghat, funeral pyres burn day and night. Families bring their loved ones here from across India, believing that cremation on these ghats grants liberation (moksha)—freedom from the cycle of rebirth.

The Eternal Flame: At Manikarnika Ghat, it is said that the fire has burned for thousands of years, tended continuously by the Doms (a caste responsible for funeral rites). This eternal flame is believed to have been lit by Lord Shiva himself. Every pyre is kindled from this sacred fire, linking each soul to an unbroken chain of spiritual continuity.

The Cycle of Life and Death: To witness these rites is to see Hindu philosophy alive in its purest form—acceptance of impermanence, reverence for the soul's journey, and the understanding that death is not an ending but a transformation.

Approaching Sacred Spaces with Respect

For travelers, seeing a cremation can be overwhelming. But it is also one of the most profound cultural encounters in Varanasi. To honor the sanctity of these spaces:

No Photography: Out of respect for grieving families, photography is strictly prohibited. This is a place of mourning, not spectacle.

Keep a Respectful Distance: Stand quietly, observe with humility, and avoid drawing attention. The rituals are not staged for tourists—they are acts of faith and love.

Silence is Reverence: Speak in whispers if at all. Allow the chants, the crackle of fire, and the river's flow to speak louder than words.

Honor the Doms' Role: The Dom community, custodians of the eternal flame, play a vital yet often marginalized role. Their service is both sacred and indispensable, deserving of respect.

The Traveler's Emotional Journey

To witness a cremation here is not an easy experience. Some travelers leave shaken, others contemplative, many profoundly moved. What unites them is a deepened awareness of life's fragility—and its beauty.

A Humbling Reminder: Standing before the eternal flame, travelers often confront their own fears of mortality. In Varanasi, death is not hidden away; it is embraced as part of existence.

Spiritual Impact: For many, the experience is transformative. Some describe feeling lighter, more present, more grateful for each moment. Others carry the quiet strength of knowing that endings are simply doorways to new beginnings.

The Gift of Perspective: Varanasi invites visitors to see life and death not as opposites, but as companions walking hand in hand along the river of time.

Closing Reflection

To walk away from Manikarnika Ghat is to carry a piece of Varanasi's eternal truth: that the flames never die, and neither does the human spirit. Here, amid ash and fire, one discovers the most luminous paradox—that death in Varanasi is not an end, but a profound continuation of life.

Chapter 7: Temples, Shrines, and Sacred Spaces

Kashi Vishwanath Temple: Heartbeat of Hindu Faith

If Varanasi is the soul of India, then the Kashi Vishwanath Temple is its beating heart. Dedicated to Lord Shiva as Vishwanath—the "Lord of the Universe"—this sacred shrine has stood for centuries as one of the most revered pilgrimage sites in Hinduism. To set foot here is to enter the very essence of Varanasi's spiritual pulse.

Architecture and Atmosphere

Golden Splendor: The temple's golden domes, plated with nearly a ton of pure gold donated by Maharaja Ranjit Singh of Punjab in the 19th century, gleam beneath the sun. In 2026, the temple complex shines brighter than ever, thanks to careful restoration and lighting that highlights its ornate spires and intricate carvings.

Sacred Energy: Inside, the air is filled with the sounds of bells, Vedic chants, and the low hum of devotees whispering prayers. The fragrance of sandalwood, incense, and marigold garlands lingers, creating an atmosphere that feels timeless and holy.

The Jyotirlinga: At its heart lies the Jyotirlinga, one of the 12 most sacred abodes of Lord Shiva. To glimpse it, even for a moment, is said to purify lifetimes of karma.

Rituals and Pilgrim Experience

Morning Mangala Aarti: At dawn, the temple comes alive with the Mangala Aarti, where priests perform an elaborate ritual to awaken the deity. The resonance of conch shells and the sight of hundreds of lamps flickering in unison leaves pilgrims awestruck.

Offerings: Devotees bring milk, honey, bilva leaves, and flowers, pouring them over the Jyotirlinga as acts of devotion.

2026 Enhancements: By now, the Kashi Vishwanath Corridor Project is fully operational, seamlessly connecting the temple to the Ganga ghats. Pilgrims enjoy smoother access, wider pathways, clean rest areas, and digital queuing systems for entry. Smart apps provide live darshan timings, translation of chants, and even AR-guided temple tours.

Practical Information for Travelers (2026)

Timings: The temple opens at 3:00 a.m. for Mangala Aarti and remains open until 11:00 p.m. Different slots exist for general darshan, special pujas, and evening rituals.

Entry Rules:

Foreigners are welcome but must adhere to dress codes—modest attire is expected (covered shoulders and knees).

No bags, cameras, or mobile phones are allowed inside. Lockers are provided outside the temple premises.

Security checks are thorough; travelers should arrive early to avoid long queues.

Tickets: General darshan is free, but special darshan passes are available for shorter waiting times. These can now be pre-booked online through the official temple portal.

Best Time to Visit: Early morning darshan (between 3–6 a.m.) offers the most serene and spiritually charged atmosphere, though evenings with the Sandhya Aarti are equally mesmerizing.

Traveler's Reflection

To stand before the Jyotirlinga is to feel the pulse of Varanasi itself. For pilgrims, it is salvation. For travelers, it is awe-inspiring. Whether you come as a seeker of faith or a student of culture, the Kashi

Vishwanath Temple offers an unforgettable glimpse into the sacred heart of Hindu devotion.

Beyond the Famous: Lesser-Known Temples and Shrines

While the Kashi Vishwanath Temple stands as the centerpiece of devotion in Varanasi, the city's true spirit lies in the countless smaller temples and shrines that line its alleys, courtyards, and ghats. Each has its own story, legend, and energy—quiet places where the rush of the world fades and the city whispers its secrets.

Hidden Temples and Their Legends

Tilbhandeshwar Mahadev Temple: Said to date back more than 2,500 years, this temple is dedicated to Lord Shiva. The linga here is believed to grow slightly in size every year—a miracle that devotees still marvel at.

Annapurna Devi Temple: Tucked near Kashi Vishwanath, this temple honors the goddess of nourishment. Legend says Shiva himself assured that no one in Kashi would ever go hungry under Annapurna's blessing.

Nepali (Kathwala) Temple: Built in traditional Nepalese pagoda style on Lalita Ghat, this 19th-century shrine resembles Kathmandu's Pashupatinath Temple. With its wooden carvings and serene riverside setting, it offers a slice of Himalayan culture in the heart of Varanasi.

Bharat Mata Temple: A unique shrine, not dedicated to a deity but to Mother India herself. Instead of idols, it houses a massive relief map of

India carved in marble—a place of patriotism and reflection.

Intimate Spiritual Experiences at Smaller Shrines

The lesser-known shrines often provide what the famous temples cannot: quiet, unhurried devotion.

You might stumble upon a priest chanting softly in a candlelit corner, with just a handful of locals joining in.

Offerings are simple—sometimes just flowers or a spoon of milk—but the connection feels deeply personal.

Travelers often report that these hidden spaces feel like stepping back into timelessness, where you can meditate or sit silently without distraction.

Thematic Temple Walks for Explorers

For those who wish to explore Varanasi through its temples, thematic walks are an ideal way to structure the journey:

Shiva Shrines Trail: From the mighty Kashi Vishwanath to smaller lingas like Tilbhandeshwar and Mrityunjay Mahadev, this walk highlights Shiva's omnipresence in Kashi.

Durga & Shakti Circuit: Visit the red Durga Kund Temple, Annapurna Devi, and smaller goddess shrines hidden in neighborhood courtyards. These spaces radiate feminine energy and devotion.

Ghatside Shrines Walk: Stroll along the Ganga from Assi to Panchganga Ghat, pausing at tiny shrines tucked between stairways and tea stalls. Each has its own tale of saints, sages, or miracles.

Cross-Cultural Temples Route: Explore the Nepali Temple, Buddhist shrines at Sarnath nearby, and Jain temples—reminders of Varanasi's plural spiritual legacy.

Traveler's Reflection

The grandeur of Varanasi is undeniable, but its soul thrives in the hidden corners. To wander into these shrines is to experience a side of the city that is raw, intimate, and often overlooked. Here, spirituality is not about spectacle, but about quiet encounters—with deities, with history, and with oneself.

Chapter 8: Cultural Treasures of Banaras

Music, Dance, and the Banaras Gharana

Varanasi is not only a city of temples and rituals—it is also a living stage where music and dance breathe life into devotion and tradition. For centuries, Banaras has nurtured some of India's greatest artists, giving rise to the Banaras Gharana, a distinctive school of Hindustani classical music and dance that continues to enchant audiences worldwide.

Music as the Soul of the City

Music in Varanasi is inseparable from its spiritual atmosphere. The sound of a sitar drifting through a narrow lane, the resonant beats of the tabla during evening gatherings, or a devotional thumri sung at dawn—all are part of the city's pulse. The Banaras Gharana, known for its powerful tabla rhythms, expressive thumri (a semi-classical vocal style), and evocative khayal performances, reflects the city's blend of discipline and emotion.

To the people of Varanasi, music is not entertainment—it is worship, meditation, and storytelling. Every note carries the weight of centuries of devotion.

Experiencing a Live Performance in 2026

In 2026, travelers can immerse themselves in performances that fuse tradition with innovation:

Ghat Concerts: Imagine sitting by the Ganges at Assi Ghat under a velvet sky, where young and senior artists perform ragas as diyas float down the river. The combination of sound, water, and fire becomes a spiritual experience.

Intimate Baithaks (gatherings): Small, candlelit courtyard concerts still thrive, where you sit cross-legged close to the musicians. The music feels personal, almost like a private conversation.

Cultural Festivals: Events such as the Ganga Mahotsav or Dhrupad Mela feature world-renowned maestros alongside rising talents, offering visitors a chance to witness the depth of Banaras artistry in full bloom.

By 2026, several cultural venues have integrated modern sound systems, live streaming, and eco-conscious event setups, allowing performances to reach global audiences without losing their traditional charm.

Where to Learn and Experience Banaras Gharana

For travelers who want more than observation, Varanasi offers places to study and connect with the living tradition:

Benares Hindu University (BHU) – Its Faculty of Performing Arts remains one of India's premier centers for training in Hindustani classical music and dance.

Pandit Ravi Shankar Institute of Music & Performing Arts – A hub for workshops, concerts, and lectures that bridge history with contemporary practice.

Smaller Gurukuls and Ashrams – Many masters still teach in traditional styles, offering one-on-one lessons in tabla, sitar, or Kathak dance for travelers who seek deeper immersion.

Cultural Cafés & Art Spaces – Modern cafés near Assi and Godowlia neighborhoods now host weekly fusion performances, where classical ragas meet jazz, Sufi music, or world instruments.

Traveler's Reflection

To experience the Banaras Gharana is to listen not just with your ears but with your spirit. In Varanasi, music is a bridge between the material and the eternal, where every raga is a prayer, and every beat of the tabla echoes the heartbeat of the city itself.

Handwoven Magic: Banarasi Silk and Craft Traditions

To walk through Varanasi is to walk through a living museum of threads. Among its most precious legacies is the Banarasi silk saree, celebrated for its intricate handwoven patterns, shimmering gold and silver zari work, and timeless elegance. More than fabric, Banarasi silk is heritage woven into cloth—a symbol of love, artistry, and identity that has adorned queens, brides, and devotees for centuries.

A Heritage of Weaving

The story of Banarasi silk dates back to the Mughal era, when Persian-inspired motifs were fused with Indian artistry. The looms of Banaras produced sarees so fine that poets described them as "woven air." Traditionally, these sarees were woven with real gold and silver threads, often taking weeks or months to complete.

Each motif carries meaning—paisleys, florals, and geometric jaals (mesh-like patterns) tell tales of prosperity, devotion, and continuity. Owning a Banarasi saree is often considered a generational treasure, passed from mother to daughter.

Meeting the Weavers

For travelers, witnessing the creation of Banarasi silk is as magical as wearing it. By 2026, several initiatives ensure ethical, immersive experiences:

Weaver's Colonies in Madanpura and Lallapura – Narrow lanes echo with the clatter of handlooms, where families continue centuries-old traditions. Travelers can sit beside artisans, watching threads transform into poetry.

Craft Tours – Guided walks introduce visitors to the life of the weavers, highlighting the challenges they face and the resilience that keeps the art alive.

Artisan Cooperatives & Studios – Places like Banaras Weavers Cooperative and women-led craft hubs allow travelers to shop directly from artisans, ensuring fair pay and preservation of heritage.

Travelers are encouraged to buy directly from these sources rather than middlemen, not only for authenticity but also to empower the communities sustaining this art.

Banarasi Silk in 2026: Tradition Meets Innovation

The silk industry has undergone transformations while remaining deeply rooted in tradition:

Technology Integration – Digital design tools assist artisans in experimenting with patterns, reducing waste, and meeting global demand without compromising on handwoven quality.

Eco-Friendly Practices – Natural dyes, organic silk threads, and solar-powered looms are increasingly common, reflecting a global shift towards sustainability.

Global Reach – Thanks to online platforms and collaborations with international designers, Banarasi silk now appears on runways in Paris, New York, and Tokyo, while still being woven in the same humble homes of Varanasi.

Revival of Crafts – Younger generations, once drifting away from weaving, are returning—motivated by fair-trade initiatives, design schools, and government programs celebrating the Banarasi heritage.

Traveler's Tip: Shopping for Authentic Banarasi Silk

Look for the GI Tag: Genuine Banarasi silk carries a Geographical Indication (GI) tag, certifying authenticity.

Price Reflects Workmanship: Handwoven sarees and dupattas require weeks of work; if a price seems too low, it's likely machine-made.

Ethical Souvenirs: Beyond sarees, travelers can find scarves, stoles, cushion covers, and wall hangings—perfect keepsakes that carry Banaras in their threads.

Reflection

To hold a Banarasi saree is to hold a fragment of eternity. Its threads connect past to present, artisans to admirers, Banaras to the world. For the mindful traveler, every purchase becomes more than a souvenir—it becomes a pledge to sustain a legacy of beauty, resilience, and devotion.

Chapter 9: A Culinary Pilgrimage

Street Food Delights: Chaat, Lassi, and Kachori

To eat in Varanasi is to experience the city with all five senses at once. Every corner, gully, and roadside stall tempts you with sizzling pans, fragrant spices, and flavors that linger long after your journey ends. For many travelers, Varanasi's street food is as sacred as its rituals—a pilgrimage of the palate.

A Symphony of Flavors

Chaat – No visit to Varanasi is complete without indulging in its famous chaat. Imagine crisp puris and fried potatoes bathed in tangy tamarind chutney, spicy green chilies, creamy yogurt, and a sprinkle of chaat masala. Each bite is sweet, sour, crunchy, and spicy all at once—a carnival in the mouth.

Lassi – Thick, frothy, and served in traditional clay cups (kulhads), Varanasi's lassi is both refreshing and indulgent. Topped with a dollop of malai (cream) and sometimes saffron or rose essence, it's the perfect antidote to a hot afternoon of exploring temples and ghats.

Kachori-Sabzi – Mornings in Varanasi often begin with kachoris—deep-fried, flaky breads stuffed with spiced lentils or peas, served with a hearty potato-tomato curry. The aroma of frying dough wafts through the alleys at dawn, inviting locals and visitors alike to gather for a breakfast ritual as old as the city itself.

Where to Eat in 2026: Local Favorites

By 2026, Varanasi's street food scene has embraced better hygiene practices while preserving its authenticity. Here are some traveler-loved stops:

Kashi Chaat Bhandar (Godowlia) – Still the gold standard for pani puri, tamatar chaat, and aloo tikki.

Blue Lassi Shop (near Manikarnika Ghat) – A legendary stop offering dozens of lassi flavors, from mango to pomegranate.

Ram Bhandar (Thatheri Bazaar) – Iconic for its kachori-sabzi breakfast—expects to queue, especially on weekends.

Deena Chaat Bhandar (Luxa Road) – Famous for creamy dahi puri and tangy tamatar chaat.

Street Stalls at Assi Ghat – A lively evening hub where travelers can taste freshly fried samosas, pakoras, and seasonal treats.

Hygiene & Dietary Tips for Travelers

Choose Busy Stalls – High turnover means fresher ingredients.

Watch the Water – Opt for bottled or filtered water; avoid ice unless you're sure it's purified.

Stick to Cooked Foods – Fried or freshly prepared items are safer than raw salads or chutneys.

Clay Cups Over Plastic – Lassi in kulhads is not only authentic but eco-friendly and safer than reused glasses.

Moderation is Key – Street food is often fried and spicy; sample in small portions to avoid stomach upsets.

Reflection

To wander Varanasi's streets is to follow the aroma of frying spices, the laughter around shared plates, and the rhythm of vendors calling out their specialties. Every bite—whether of a crisp kachori or a creamy lassi—isn't just food, but a story, a memory, and a connection to the soul of the city.

Dining with a View: Riverside Cafés and Rooftop Restaurants

If the streets of Varanasi are alive with energy and flavor, the rooftops and riverside cafés are its quiet sanctuaries. By 2026, the city's skyline along the Ganges has transformed into a tapestry of intimate rooftop terraces and atmospheric eateries, where travelers can pause, dine, and take in breathtaking views of the river's timeless flow.

Dining with the Ganges as Your Backdrop

Rooftop Cafés – As the sun sets, the ghats below begin to glow with lamps and chants, while rooftops fill with soft music, warm lanterns, and the aroma of simmering curries or Italian pasta. The vantage point offers a magical balance: the bustle of Varanasi below, serenity of the river beyond.

Riverside Lounges – Some modern cafés now spill onto terraces just above the water, where fairy lights twinkle, bamboo décor creates a rustic charm, and travelers sip masala chai or craft cocktails while boats drift past.

Popular & Emerging Spots in 2026

Shiva Café & German Bakery (near Assi Ghat) – A backpacker favorite for years, now updated with organic options and live music nights.

Varuna Rooftop (Godowlia area) – Known for its fusion menu—think wood-fired pizza beside North Indian thalis—paired with panoramic river views.

Open Hand Café (Bengali Tola) – A socially conscious café supporting local artisans, serving great coffee and continental breakfasts with soulful rooftop seating.

The Ganges View Lounge (near Munshi Ghat) – A boutique riverside restaurant perfect for couples, offering candlelit dinners with curated Indian tasting menus.

Emerging Assi Ghat Spaces (2026) – New eco-conscious rooftop eateries here combine bamboo interiors, acoustic folk nights, and menus featuring farm-to-table Banarasi dishes with a global twist.

Vibe & Ambiance

Morning – Sip a cappuccino or fresh lime soda as the mist rises from the river, listening to the gentle lapping of boats and distant temple bells.

Evening – Rooftops glow with string lights, soft sitar or indie acoustic sets create a calming mood, and you can watch the flickering lamps of the Ganga Aarti from above.

Late Night – Some cafés stay open late, offering travelers a place to gather, share stories, and soak in the peaceful river under starlit skies.

Dining Recommendations

For Authentic Indian – Order a traditional thali platter with dal, sabzi, rice, and roti while watching the river slowly turn golden at sunset.

For Fusion Lovers – Try tandoori paneer pizzas, masala hummus wraps, or Banarasi-inspired pasta.

For Light Bites – Smoothie bowls, fresh salads, and herbal teas are increasingly popular among wellness-conscious travelers.

Reflection

Eating on a rooftop in Varanasi is more than dining—it's meditation through the senses. As you savor flavors both local and global, the river below reminds you of continuity, while the city around you hums with life. Few meals in the world offer such a blend of taste, atmosphere, and spiritual presence.

Chapter 10: Festivals of Fire and Color

Dev Deepawali: The Festival of a Thousand Lamps

Few spectacles in the world compare to Dev Deepawali in Varanasi, when the sacred Ganges is transformed into a river of light. Held on the full moon night of Kartik (usually in November), this festival honors the gods' descent to the earth. By 2026, Dev Deepawali has grown into an even grander celebration, with eco-friendly practices and improved crowd management making the experience more vibrant and welcoming than ever.

The Magic of a Thousand Lamps

As twilight falls, thousands of diyas (oil lamps) are lit along the steps of over 80 ghats. Their golden glow reflects on the water, creating the illusion of a sky of stars mirrored in the river. The air hums with the sound of conch shells, temple bells, and chanting. Boats, decorated with flowers and lanterns, drift slowly across the river, offering travelers a floating view of this cosmic spectacle.

For locals, lighting diyas is an offering of devotion to the Ganga and the gods; for travelers, it's a chance to step into a timeless ritual, blending awe with serenity.

Participation in 2026

For Locals – Families gather on the ghats, lighting lamps, offering prayers, and singing bhajans late into the night. Many neighborhoods also organize cultural performances—classical dance, folk singing, and plays that narrate mythological stories.

For Travelers – In 2026, several ghats now have designated visitor sections where travelers can safely light diyas under guidance, ensuring they can participate respectfully. Eco-friendly clay lamps and biodegradable oils are widely available to reduce waste. Boat tours also include lamp-lighting experiences, letting you release floating diyas into the river.

Best Ghats to Experience Dev Deepawali

Dasashwamedh Ghat – The grandest and busiest, with massive crowds and the most elaborate rituals. Ideal for those who want to feel the full intensity.

Assi Ghat – More spacious, popular with young locals and travelers, featuring music and cultural performances.

Panchganga Ghat – Known for its spiritual calm, great for a more reflective and less crowded experience.

Riverside by Boat – Perhaps the most magical vantage point, where you float between illuminated ghats and see the whole city shimmering.

Practical Tips (2026)

Timing – Lamps are lit at sunset, but arrive by 4–5 pm to secure a good spot. The celebrations continue into late evening.

Safety – Stick to designated visitor areas on the ghats, as the steps can be slippery and crowded. Boats are regulated in 2026 with stricter safety standards, so work only with licensed operators.

What to Bring – Comfortable walking shoes, a shawl or light jacket (November evenings can be cool), and a power bank for your camera or phone.

Respect – Participate with reverence—avoid blocking rituals or using flash photography when close to ceremonies.

Reflection: Dev Deepawali is not just a festival of light—it's a festival of perspective. Standing by the river, you realize that each diya represents both an individual prayer and a collective illumination. For travelers, it's an unforgettable moment of feeling part of something eternal, where tradition and modernity glow side by side.

Holi in Banaras: Colors of Joy and Spiritual Play

If Dev Deepawali is Varanasi's festival of light, then Holi is its festival of life itself—loud, unrestrained, and gloriously messy. By March, the ghats, lanes, and rooftops of Banaras explode into a kaleidoscope of powders, laughter, music, and dance. Holi here is not just play—it's a spiritual celebration of good over evil, of community over isolation, and of joy as a form of devotion.

The Vibrant Chaos of Banaras Holi

In Banaras, Holi begins days before the actual date, with bonfires of Holika Dahan marking the victory of light over darkness. On the main day, the entire city becomes a playground:

Children hurl gulal (colored powders) and water balloons from rooftops.

Musicians parade through the lanes, playing drums and singing folk songs.

Strangers embrace as friends, greeting each other with "Holi hai!"

The ghats transform into open-air arenas where devotees, students, and travelers join in a blur of dance, song, and colors.

Unlike in some cities, Banaras' Holi is deeply tied to its spiritual roots. Temples host special pujas, and the colors are seen as symbolic offerings to the gods. Some neighborhoods observe Lathmar Holi (playful stick fights between men and women) or community feasts where bhaang (a cannabis-based drink mixed with milk) adds a hint of mischievous energy to the day.

What Makes Banaras Holi Unique

Temple Rituals – The celebration is interwoven with visits to shrines, where colored powders are offered to deities before being shared among devotees.

The Ghats – Few places in India offer the surreal experience of playing Holi by the Ganges, with colors drifting into the sacred waters.

Inclusivity – Locals often invite travelers into their homes to celebrate, turning strangers into instant family.

Tips for Travelers (2026)

Safety First – Stick to busy public areas or celebrate with locals you trust. Some alleys can get rowdy, so avoid isolated lanes.

Protect Yourself – Wear old clothes you don't mind discarding, oil your hair and skin beforehand to make washing off easier, and use protective eyewear for sensitive eyes.

Photography – Keep your camera or phone in a waterproof pouch. Wide shots of crowds on the ghats or candid portraits of powdered faces make for the most memorable frames.

Mind the Bhaang – Popular during Holi, this drink can be stronger than expected. Enjoy it in moderation and only from trusted sources.

Respect the Spirit – Holi is playful, but always set your boundaries politely. A simple "No, thank you" with a smile goes a long way.

Reflection: Holi in Banaras is not about color alone—it's about surrender. You surrender to laughter, to strangers becoming companions, to music filling your body, to the chaos that somehow feels like order. For many travelers, it's the moment they stop observing the city and finally become part of it.

Chapter 11: Day Trips and Excursions Beyond Varanasi

Sarnath: In the Footsteps of the Buddha

Just a short journey from the chaos and chants of Varanasi lies Sarnath, one of the most sacred Buddhist sites in the world. Here, in the Deer Park (Rishipattana), the Buddha gave his first sermon after attaining enlightenment in Bodh Gaya, setting into motion the Dharma Chakra—the "Wheel of Law." For centuries, monks, pilgrims, and seekers from across Asia have journeyed here, and in 2026,

Sarnath remains a living spiritual center where silence and devotion seem to saturate the air.

A Sacred Atmosphere in 2026

Sarnath balances the serenity of history with modern touches designed for global travelers:

Dhamek Stupa still towers at the heart of the site, its massive cylindrical stone base weathered yet timeless, marking the spot where the Buddha preached. Pilgrims walk in meditative circles around it, murmuring chants or turning prayer wheels.

Mulagandha Kuti Vihara, built by the Mahabodhi Society, fills the space with incense, gilded statues, and frescoes that depict the Buddha's life. Daily prayers and chanting continue to draw both monks and curious visitors.

The Sarnath Museum, recently digitized, now offers interactive displays alongside ancient sculptures—including the famous Lion Capital of Ashoka, India's national emblem.

Meditation gardens and retreat centers in 2026 welcome travelers to pause, sit, and simply be—an antidote to the intensity of Varanasi's ghats.

The atmosphere feels contemplative: monks in saffron robes, the rustle of Bodhi trees, and the rhythmic toll of temple bells blend into a symphony of stillness.

Practical Advice for Travelers

Getting There: Sarnath lies about 10 km northeast of Varanasi. Auto-rickshaws, taxis, and app-based rideshares make the trip in 30–40 minutes. Group tours often include Sarnath as a half-day excursion.

Entry & Fees (2026): The Sarnath Archaeological Site and Museum has a modest entry fee (around ₹50 for Indians, ₹300 for foreigners). Children under 15 usually enter free. Most temples and monasteries are open without charge but accept donations.

Timings: The museum is open from 9 AM to 5 PM, closed on Fridays. The archaeological park opens from sunrise to sunset. Early mornings and late afternoons are the most peaceful times to visit.

Best Way to Experience: Consider hiring a licensed guide at the entrance—they bring centuries of stories to life. For spiritual travelers, joining a guided meditation session in one of the monasteries adds depth to the visit.

Reflection: Where Varanasi's ghats confront you with life and death in vivid immediacy, Sarnath invites you inward, into the quiet revolution of compassion and awareness that the Buddha first taught here. A day in Sarnath is not just an excursion—it's a step into the unfolding journey of inner peace.

Rural Escapes: Villages, Weaving Centers, and Countryside Life

Just beyond the bustling ghats of Varanasi lies another world—the quiet countryside of Eastern Uttar Pradesh, where time seems to move with the rhythm of the seasons. Visiting a rural village here in 2026 offers a refreshing contrast to the intensity of the city: mud-walled houses painted with natural colors, fields of sugarcane and wheat swaying in the wind, and the laughter of children running barefoot along narrow paths.

The Village Experience

Stepping into a village near Varanasi is like entering a living museum of tradition:

Hospitality: Guests are often welcomed with a smile, a cup of fresh chai, or even homemade sweets like gur (jaggery) treats. Rural families take pride in sharing their culture and often invite travelers into their courtyards.

Traditions: Daily life follows an age-old rhythm—farmers tending fields at sunrise, women weaving or cooking on clay stoves, elders gathering under banyan trees to share stories. Seasonal festivals bring vibrant processions, folk songs, and communal meals.

Crafts: Many villages around Varanasi are linked to weaving, especially Banarasi silk. Travelers can watch artisans at handlooms, their fingers dancing across threads of gold and silk. Some villages also specialize in pottery, woodwork, or folk painting.

Weaving Centers and Craft Heritage

Sarai Mohana, a weaving village, is famous for its Banarasi saris. Here, artisans often welcome visitors into their workshops, demonstrating centuries-old techniques while also explaining how modern technology (like jacquard looms) has blended into the craft by 2026.

Purchasing directly from artisans ensures fair wages and helps keep traditions alive. Many workshops now provide certificates of authenticity to distinguish handwoven silks from machine-made copies.

Ethical and Sustainable Rural Tours

In 2026, rural tourism has evolved to prioritize community benefit and cultural sensitivity:

Village Homestays: Some families open their homes to visitors, offering simple but warm accommodations with home-cooked meals made from farm-fresh produce.

Community-Based Tours: Organizations and NGOs arrange guided experiences that support education, healthcare, or craft cooperatives. Fees go directly back to the village.

Responsible Travel Tips: Dress modestly, ask before taking photographs, and avoid handing out money or sweets directly to children—instead, support schools or women's collectives.

Reflection: A day in the countryside reminds travelers that India's heart still beats strongest in its villages. Here, amidst humble homes and handwoven magic, you discover the values of simplicity, resilience, and community that have shaped Varanasi for centuries.

Chapter 12: Modern Varanasi – 2026 and Beyond

Smart City Developments: Infrastructure and Traveler Experience

Varanasi may be one of the world's oldest living cities, but by 2026 it is also one of India's leading Smart Cities—a place where heritage and innovation meet on the ghats of the Ganges. For travelers, this means smoother arrivals, easier navigation, and safer, more connected experiences without losing the essence of Banaras' timeless charm.

Upgraded Infrastructure

Air Travel: The Lal Bahadur Shastri International Airport has been expanded with new international terminals, offering direct connections to Southeast Asia, Europe, and the Middle East. Faster immigration e-gates make arrivals more seamless.

Metro & Electric Mobility: The Varanasi Metro (launched in phases, now fully operational by 2026) links the airport, railway station, and key ghats. E-rickshaws and shared electric shuttles reduce congestion in old city lanes while cutting down on pollution.

Smart Roads & River Transport: Digital signboards, traffic sensors, and an upgraded river transport system now allow eco-friendly ferries across the Ganges—an efficient alternative to road traffic.

Technology Meets Tradition

Digital Pilgrimage: Apps like Kashi Connect provide live temple schedules, queue-booking for darshan at Kashi Vishwanath, and guided AR (augmented reality) tours of ancient sites.

Cashless Transactions: From street chai stalls to silk showrooms, UPI payments and e-wallets are universal, meaning travelers rarely need to carry large sums of cash.

Sustainability Features: Solar-powered street lighting, eco-monitoring systems for Ganga water quality, and smart waste management make the city cleaner and more eco-conscious than ever before.

Traveler Hacks for 2026

Transport Apps: Use Varanasi Metro App and E-Rickshaw Connect to plan routes, avoid overcharging, and estimate real-time fares.

Language Help: AI-driven translation tools are integrated into local travel apps—perfect for communicating with rickshaw drivers or market vendors.

Cultural AR Guides: Download AR-enabled walking tour apps to see reconstructions of temples, Mughal ghats, or Buddha's sermon at Sarnath as you stand on location.

Emergency Access: One-tap SOS features in travel apps link you directly to tourist police and emergency services.

Balancing Tourism with Tradition: Sustainable and Responsible Travel

Varanasi has always carried the weight of eternity on its ghats—but by 2026, it also carries the weight of millions of annual visitors. The city's challenge has been clear: how to welcome the world while protecting its fragile cultural fabric and sacred river. The answer lies in balance—between tourism and tradition, progress and preservation.

Managing Overtourism

Regulated Ghats: Authorities now manage crowd flow during peak rituals such as the Ganga Aarti, introducing timed entry zones and dedicated boat lanes to prevent overcrowding.

Temple Management Systems: Popular temples like Kashi Vishwanath have digital queuing systems and booking slots, ensuring smoother pilgrim experiences without overwhelming priests or worshippers.

Community-Based Tourism: Local guides, homestays, and neighborhood initiatives encourage visitors to spread out across less-touristed areas, easing pressure on iconic sites.

Eco-Conscious Practices for Travelers

Plastic-Free Pilgrimage: Single-use plastics are banned along the ghats; travelers are encouraged to carry reusable bottles and cloth bags.

Water Respect: Avoid polluting the Ganges—do not throw flowers, food, or offerings unless they are biodegradable and placed in designated eco-baskets.

Low-Impact Transport: Choose walking, cycling, or e-rickshaws within the old city rather than fuel-based vehicles. Boats powered by solar and biofuel are widely available and recommended.

Mindful Consumption: Support eateries and cafes that adopt farm-to-table sourcing and avoid food waste.

Leaving a Positive Footprint

Support Local Artisans: Buying authentic Banarasi silk directly from weavers' cooperatives helps preserve age-old traditions.

Join Clean-Up Drives: Many NGOs and youth groups organize riverbank clean-ups—visitors can volunteer for a few hours.

Respect Rituals: Observe with humility—photograph sensitively, dress modestly, and avoid interrupting ceremonies.

Give Back: Contribute to local schools, cultural preservation projects, or eco-initiatives rather than offering random handouts that disrupt community balance.

Takeaway:
Varanasi thrives when visitors become custodians, not just consumers. By traveling with awareness—honoring the river, respecting rituals, and uplifting local communities—you don't just witness the soul of the city, you help protect it for generations to come.

Chapter 13: Reflections – Leaving with the Spirit of Varanasi

Lessons from the Ghats: What Varanasi Teaches Travelers

To walk the ghats of Varanasi is to step into a classroom without walls, where every ritual, chant, and sunrise whispers lessons that linger long after you leave. The city is more than stone steps and sacred waters—it is a living mirror, showing travelers not only what India holds sacred but also what life itself asks of us.

The Lesson of Impermanence

Watching funeral pyres burn at Manikarnika Ghat, travelers confront life's most certain truth: everything ends. Yet, in the rising smoke, there is no despair—only release, acceptance, and continuity. Varanasi teaches that endings are not to be feared but honored as part of the great cycle.

The Lesson of Devotion

At Dasashwamedh Ghat, where fire dances in priests' hands during the evening Ganga Aarti, devotion shines as a force greater than spectacle. It's a reminder that whether one bows to a god, an idea, or the river itself, the act of surrender deepens our humanity.

The Lesson of Simplicity

A quiet dawn boat ride across the Ganges reminds us that the most profound beauty often lies in simplicity—the oar cutting through still waters, the saffron of the sun touching temple spires, the sound of bells echoing over the city. In those small moments, life feels both vast and intimate.

The Lesson of Reflection

In Varanasi's winding alleys, travelers encounter not just shrines and shopkeepers but also themselves. The city does not flatter; it reveals. Its chaos can mirror your restlessness, its stillness your longing for peace. To be here is to be challenged, but also to be clarified.

Traveler's Reflection: One visitor put it best after days on the ghats: "Varanasi didn't give me answers. It gave me perspective. And sometimes that's all you need."

In the end, Varanasi leaves you with lessons not tied to religion or geography but to the shared human experience: to live fully, to let go gracefully, and to recognize the sacred in the everyday.

Taking the Light Home: Carrying Varanasi Into Everyday Life

Leaving Varanasi does not mean leaving its spirit behind. The ghats, the river, and the timeless rituals stay with you, quietly reshaping the way you walk through your own days. The city's greatest gift is not just what you witnessed, but what you carry forward.

Mindfulness in the Everyday

Just as the Ganges flows steadily, travelers can invite presence into ordinary moments—pausing before meals, taking a few breaths at sunrise, or walking more slowly through familiar streets. Varanasi teaches us that each small act, when done with awareness, becomes sacred.

The Beauty of Simplicity

A clay cup of chai sipped on the ghats reminds us that joy often comes in unadorned forms. At home, it might mean lighting a candle at the end of the day, preparing food with intention, or simply savoring silence without rushing to fill it.

Reverence for Life's Cycles

The eternal flame of Manikarnika shows us the dignity of beginnings and endings. Travelers can honor this lesson by embracing change without fear—celebrating arrivals, grieving departures, and trusting the rhythm of their own journey.

Small Rituals to Keep the Spirit Alive

Begin the day with five minutes of stillness, as if greeting your own inner sunrise.

Carry a small journal, jotting down moments of gratitude or reflection, the way pilgrims carry offerings.

Create your own "ghat" at home—a corner with a candle, flower, or bowl of water—as a space for grounding and renewal.

Closing Reflection

Varanasi does not ask you to stay forever—it asks you to live differently when you return. To see your own city, your own life, as alive with meaning. To treat each encounter, each breath, each turning of the day as holy.

When you carry this light forward, you are no longer just a traveler who visited Varanasi. You become part of its living story. And perhaps, in your own way, you will inspire others to seek their river, their awakening, their eternal flame.

Conclusion

Every journey has an ending, yet some places never truly let you go. Varanasi is one of them. It clings to you—not as a memory, but as a mirror, reflecting truths you may have forgotten about yourself.

On the ghats, you witnessed fire and water in eternal dialogue—life, death, and rebirth woven into every flame and ripple. In the temples, you felt devotion rising like incense, ancient yet alive in each chant. In the alleys, you touched the pulse of a city that thrives in both chaos and grace.

Varanasi is not a destination; it is an awakening. It whispers that time is fleeting, yet every moment can be sacred. It reminds you that simplicity—whether in a clay cup of chai, a soft sunrise, or the quiet kindness of a stranger—holds more beauty than the grandest luxuries. And it teaches that endings, like the cremation flames, are not to be feared but honored, for they make space for beginnings.

As you close this guide, know that you are carrying more than travel notes. You are carrying light. Perhaps you will light a candle at home and remember the river glowing with diyas. Perhaps you will pause before a meal and hear echoes of temple bells. Or perhaps you will simply breathe, more slowly, knowing that life is not a race but a pilgrimage.

The spirit of Varanasi is yours to keep—quietly shaping how you love, how you live, how you see the sacred in the everyday. And when you return, as so many travelers do, you will not be the same person who first arrived.

Varanasi is not just a city you visit.
It is a city that visits you—
and stays with you, forever.

Printed in Dunstable, United Kingdom